# DESTINY

## Florence Espeut-Nickless

T0353274

*methuen* | drama

LONDON · NEW YORK · OXFORD · NEW DELHI · SYDNEY

METHUEN DRAMA
Bloomsbury Publishing Plc
50 Bedford Square, London, WC1B 3DP, UK
1385 Broadway, New York, NY 10018, USA
29 Earlsfort Terrace, Dublin 2, Ireland

BLOOMSBURY, METHUEN DRAMA and the Methuen
Drama logo are trademarks of Bloomsbury Publishing Plc

First published in Great Britain 2022

Cover design by Jade Barnett

Cover photograph © Paul Blakemore

A catalogue record for this book is available from the British Library.

A catalog record for this book is available from the Library of Congress.

ISBN: PB: 978-1-3503-5419-7
ePDF: 978-1-3503-5420-3
eBook: 978-1-3503-5421-0

Series: Modern Plays

Typeset by Mark Heslington Ltd, Scarborough, North Yorkshire

To find out more about our authors and books visit
www.bloomsbury.com and sign up for our newsletters.

Hi, I'm Florence.

I grew up on a council estate in Chippenham in the noughties.

*DESTINY* is inspired by mine and my mate's experiences in that place and time

By the challenges we faced

The systems we had to fight against

The dreams we lost

And the ones we desperately held onto.

It's ultimately a celebration of working class resilience, drive and determination, of fighting against our destiny and reaching for the mf stars!

## Acknowledgements

It's taken a lot of time, hustle, commitment, generosity and love from so many people and organisations to get *DESTINY* here . . .

Tom, Jesse, Jen, Joe, Vic, Tim, Jenny – a true dream team. Love and gratitude forever! So blessed you came on this journey with me.

My incredible agents at Curtis Brown, Jessica Cooper and Gemma Craig, thanks for literally everything, for helping me believe I can do shit, when I don't feel like I can – beyond lucky!

My beautiful mad family, thanks for the love, the chaos, the ride. Thanks for giving me too much shit to write about! Too many of you to shout out. But you know I love you all innit! Thanks for always believing. Could not do this without you all behind me.

Gotta do a few special fam mentions though . . .

Tadgh, thanks for being by my side the last couple of years. For always sitting on the back row. For making me laugh when I need it. For keeping me calm when I feel overwhelmed. Legit, would've crumbled without you.

Ned, thanks for standing at the back with your camera, for filming all the scratch nights, so many scratch nights! And for making us all look mad sexy in the photos!

Michelle, thanks for sharing your social worker knowledge and wisdom with us. And for doing what you do, for countless Destiny's out there. So much respect!

My Chippenham girls, thanks for all the magic and mayhem over the years! And mostly thank you for letting me tell your story as well as mine. You're the true stars innit!

My Bristol babes. Thanks for being here through all the madness, could not have done the last decade without you around. You inspire, challenge and crack me up on the daily. The respect and love runs deep honeys.

Dom O'Hanlon and all at Methuen Drama, thanks for this opportunity. For helping Destiny's story live on.

Big shout out to the following people and organisations, thanks for it all – the time, space, belief, support . . .

Tobacco Factory Theatres, Bristol Old Vic FERMENT, Strike A Light, Pentabus Theatre, Wild Child, Pound Arts, The Pleasance, Tim Crouch, Wiltshire Creative, Natural Theatre, Theatre Bristol, Paper Arts, Gane Trust, Hawkwood College, Tender, Arts Council England, Oliver Lansley, Christa Harris, Daisy Douglas, Lauren Gauge, Emile Clarke, Robert Turton, Clemency Calkin, Madi Mahoney, Suhayla El Bushra, Matthew Emeny, Rina Vergano, Gemma Brooks and Jean Goubert.

To everyone that's so generously donated to our Edinburgh Crowdfunder. Forever grateful xxx

# DESTINY

Written and performed by Florence Espeut-Nickless
Director: Jesse Jones
Dramaturg: Tim Crouch and Jesse Jones
Composer and Sound Designer: Joseff Harris
Lighting Designer and Production Manager: Jenny Roxburgh
Producer and Tour Manager: Tom Bevan
Original Producer: Victoria Hole
Associate Director: Jenny Davies

*DESTINY* is a recipient of The Pleasance's 2021 National Partnerships Award with Bristol Old Vic FERMENT and was shortlisted for Theatre West's Write On Women Award. It has been developed with support from Tobacco Factory Theatres, Bristol Old Vic FERMENT, Pound Arts, Strike A Light, Pentabus Theatre, The Pleasance, Tim Crouch, Wiltshire Creative, Natural Theatre, Paper Arts, Theatre Bristol, Hawkwood College, Arts Council England and Gane Trust.

## Creative Team

# Florence Espeut-Nickless – Writer and Performer

Florence is a writer and actor from Chippenham in Wiltshire, a town with no theatre and limited access to it. She writes for both stage and screen about and with working class communities in the Southwest in the hope of making the arts more accessible to everyone, regardless of background and geographical location. She is the CRF Writer in Residence at Pentabus Theatre, an Open Session Writer at Bristol Old Vic and an associate artist at Strike A Light, as part of the Let Artists Be Artists programme.

DESTINY is her debut play. It was a recipient of the Pleasance 2021 National Partnerships Award (with Bristol Old Vic Ferment) and shortlisted for Theatre West's Write On Women Award. It is currently in development for digital and TV versions with Pentabus, Rural Media and Wild Child.

Florence was commissioned to write *Miracle on 34 Seymour Street* for Trowbridge Town Hall over Christmas 2021 (with songwriter Gavin Osborn). She is developing another play, *Blinded By Your Grace*, with support from MAYK, Strike A Light, Wiltshire Creative and Tobacco Factory Theatres. Florence is also one of five writers working on the re-telling of *The Odyssey* with the National Theatre (for Trowbridge Town Hall).

# Victoria Hole – Original Producer

Vic has worked for Bristol Old Vic, The Tobacco Factory Theatre (TFT), MAYK, the egg, Take Art, Theatre Orchard. Producing credits include *Champ* and *The Borrowers* (TFT); *Much Ado About Puffin* (Open Attic Company) and DESTINY (Florence Espeut-Nickless). Vic is now managing a conservation project for the Wildlife Trust.

# Jesse Jones – Director and Dramaturg

Jesse Jones is a theatre director from Bristol. He is a founding member of award-winning company The Wardrobe Ensemble who are associates of Complicité and Shoreditch Town Hall; they have toured nationally and internationally. Jesse was Resident Director at Royal & Derngate, Northampton having won the Regional Theatre

Young Directors Scheme award. He is also alumni of the Old Vic 12, NT directors program and Bristol Old Vic's made in Bristol scheme. In 2011 Jesse founded the Wardrobe Theatre where he was Artistic Director until 2015, before leaving he helped establish the theatre as the leading fringe theatre in the city. He is now also a trustee of Shoreditch Town Hall.

Recent credits include: *Sorry, You're Not a Winner* (Paines Plough and Theatre Royal Plymouth); *Winners* (The Wardrobe Ensemble); *Death Drop* (The Garrick Theatre – Trafalgar Entertainment); *The Last of the Pelican Daughters* (Complicité/Royal & Derngate/Bristol Old Vic); *Pippi Longstocking* (Royal & Derngate/York Theatre Royal/Wizard Presents); *Education, Education, Education* (Royal & Derngate/Shoreditch Town Hall/The Wardrobe Ensemble, Winner of a Stage Award & Scotsman Fringe First).

## Tim Crouch – Dramaturg

Tim is an Obie-award winning writer, director, performer and theatre-maker. His plays include *My Arm, An Oak Tree, ENGLAND, The Author, I, Malvolio, I, Cinna (the poet), Adler & Gibb, Beginners, Total Immediate Collective Imminent Terrestrial Salvation, Superglue* and *Truth's a Dog Must to Kennel*. Tim created and co-wrote *Don't Forget the Driver*, a six-part series for BBC2 which won Best TV Comedy at the Venice TV awards, 2019.

## Joseff Harris – Composer and Sound Designer

Joseff Harris is a composer, sound designer and audio producer working across theatre, film and audio. He is interested in how sound can tap into our subconscious, seeking to create work that transports us to vivid worlds. He draws upon eclectic influences to create compelling scores often interwoven with sounds from the natural world. Joseff also releases music under his own name, with his debut EP Talking to Trees being released last year and featuring on national radio stations.

Recent and upcoming credits include: *Macbeth* (Royal Birmingham Conservatoire); *Galapagos* (Central School of Speech & Drama); *If. Destroyed. Still. True.* (Jawbones Theatre); *Miracle on 34 Seymour Street* (Trowbridge Town Hall); *Assembling* (Tim Lytc and Knowle West Media Centre); *Atlantis* (Arts at the Old Fire Station); *See*

*Monster* (New Substance); *Weathering Together* (Theatre Orchard); *underGrowth* (BBC Radio 4).

## Jenny Roxburgh – Lighting Designer

Jen's enjoyed lighting productions with companies that produce theatre to inspire and broaden the perspective of audiences. Her design path started when she was awarded the BBC Performing Arts Ones to Watch fellowship in Lighting Design with English Touring Theatre. Her most recent designs include *DESTINY*, created by Florence Espeut-Nickless performing at Tobacco Factory Theatre, and the production of *Cockroach*, written and performed by Chloe Mantripp at Jacksons Lane. Other work includes designing and installing the lights for a new cafe and bookshop in St Paul's, Bristol called Hidden Corner, *Look, No Hands* at The Pleasance Theatre in London written and performed by Lila Clements, and Postcard Production's *The Stranger on the Bridge* at the Tobacco Factory Theatre.

Check out her website at *www.jenlroxburgh.com/*

## Tom Bevan – Producer

Tom is a freelance producer from Cardiff, based in Bristol. He has worked in teams across different scale of organisations, including Theatr Clwyd (Assistant Producer), Battersea Arts Centre (Co-Creating Change Project Manager), Dirty Protest (Producer), Strike A Light and Coventry City of Culture (Producer, Hungry Nation) and Cardiff Council (Arts Programmer, Summer of Smiles). He is a fundraiser and tour manager for individual theatre artists and musicians and has taken work to several Edinburgh Fringe and VAULT Festivals.

He is interested in new writing, long-term artist development and work that is co-created. Tom is passionate about healthy working conditions in the arts; he wants to create environments where people can thrive.

## Jenny Davies – Associate Director

Jenny Davies is a UK based director and theatre-maker. In 2019 she was awarded the prestigious Leverhulme Arts Scholarship through

Bristol Old Vic and was Resident Assistant Director at Tobacco Factory Theatres 2018-19.

Her recent directing credits include *Outlier* (Bristol Old Vic), *Hamelin* (the egg, Theatre Royal Bath), *Miracle on 34 Seymour Street* (Trowbridge Town Hall), *The Waiting Room* (the egg, Theatre Royal Bath). Jenny is Associate Director of the West End drag murder mystery show, *Death Drop*, which toured across the UK in 2021. She is co-founder of Propolis Theatre, a company formed out of the Bristol Old Vic 'Made In Bristol' scheme and a member of Interval Artists' Collective.

*DESTINY* was made possible by so many people and partners. These four organisations have been instrumental in the development of the show.

# TOBACCO FACTORY THEATRES

**Tobacco Factory Theatres** produces and presents excellent art in unique, intimate spaces at Tobacco Factory Theatres in Bristol, as well as off site in Bristol and in venues across the country. It presents a jam-packed programme of diverse and exciting shows, workshops and events, from classic and contemporary theatre, to theatre for families, comedy, dance, music, opera and puppetry. It also runs an expanding programme of engagement, learning and participation opportunities for audiences, artists and young people.

Tobacco Factory Theatres has forged an inspirational path to becoming one of the country's most respected venues. The diversity of the programme, combined with the astonishing average attendance capacity of 84%, make it one of the most well-attended, loved and popular theatres in the country.

*tobaccofactorytheatres.com*

**BRISTOL OLD VIC FERMENT**

**Bristol Old Vic** is the oldest continuously working theatre in the English speaking world, built in 1766 as a place where the people of Bristol could come together, It was built as a symbol of the pride we have in our city and what it can achieve and remains a place of joy, discovery and adventure to this day. Our mission is to create pioneering twenty-first-century theatre in partnership with the people of our energetic city; inspired by the history and magical design of the most beautiful playhouse in the country.

Ferment is the name we give to our New Work programme supporting artists and companies based in/from the South West. It has been running for more than ten years, and in that time we have worked with hundreds of artists to explore new ideas, grow their creative practice, and develop shows/projects that have gone on to tour nationally and internationally.

We target our work specifically towards the development of *entry-level, early and mid-career artists*. We identify and support artists and companies through a mixture of open-access opportunities, open calls and curation.

*bristololdvic.org.uk*

**Strike A Light**

At Strike A Light, we create events that people never imagined would or could happen in their city. We tell people's stories through performance and create brilliant participation opportunities for young people.

Gloucester is a diverse city and we make sure that the people we work with, the shows we programme and the companies we support reflect this.

We believe that the arts can change lives and that *everyone*, regardless of background and circumstance, should be given opportunities to watch, make and participate.

So far, Strike A Light have welcomed thousands of audience members, supported dozens of performers and companies to create new shows and given hundreds of young people the chance to take part in arts activities – often for the first time.

Audiences have danced on rooftops, made a meal for 100 people, been part of a National Theatre show, explored Gloucester's housing estates with a group of teenagers, become part of a flashmob, eaten fish and chips while young people performed a beatbox show and watched high quality national touring work in empty shops, churches, community centres, schools and Gloucester streets.

*Strikealight.org.uk*

# PENTABUS

Pentabus is the nation's rural theatre company. We are the only professional theatre company in the UK whose vision is singularly rural. We tour new plays about the contemporary rural world to audiences in village halls, fields, festivals and theatres, telling stories with local relevance, plus national and international impact. We believe that every person living in an isolated rural community has a right to exceptional theatre. We are based in a Victorian school in rural Shropshire, and to date all of our work has been made here. It then tours village halls and theatres locally and nationally. Over four and a half decades we've produced 174 new plays, reached over half a million audience members, won a prestigious South Bank Show award, a Fringe First and were the first to live stream from a village hall. We have hosted a writer in residence since 2014 and they have gone on to be commissioned by the Birmingham Repertory Theatre, Bush Theatre, HighTide, Nottingham Playhouse, National Theatre, Royal Court and Royal Welsh College.

We are a champion for rural young people aged 16 to 25 and Pentabus Young Company is our programme offering workshops, work experience and mentorships, as well as the opportunity to join our Young Writers' Group, which has been running for nine years.

www.pentabus.co.uk

*DESTINY.* Get involved.

Join the conversation.

Twitter: @FlorenceEN

Instagram: @florenceespeutnickless

Facebook: @DESTINYFlorenceEN

If you are affected by any of the issues in *DESTINY* support is available.

You can talk to the Samaritans right now on 116 123 (24/7 free helpline).

www.samaritans.org

www.thesurvivorstrust.org – links to national and local support services

www.womensaid.org.uk

# DESTINY

*For Chippenham*

*For Hill Rise*

*For all the Destiny's out there young & old*
*Keep shining babes*
*We see you*

*For my fam, my mates, my team*
*For holding my hand through this*
*For celebrating the wins*
*For wiping the tears*
*For sticking with me even when I took 2 weeks to reply to a text*

*Got u 4L*

*Flo x*

**Character**

**Destiny,** *girl – age 15–16 – Wiltshire accent*

**1 – Club**

*'Crazy In Love' by Beyonce ft. Jay Z plays.*

It's Thursday night
Me an Gem
Tonight's gonna be a big night!
It's WTF 50 down Karma
All drinks 50p. All night
So 10 Smirnoff Ices is like . . . well cheap

It's hands down the best night out in Chippenham.
No word of a lie
Actually on second thoughts probably the whole of Wiltshire
An Wiltshire's pretty big ya know
Swindon, Trowbridge an Melksham
Basically everywhere, except Bristol, but Bristol's massive so
that don't count
An Bath? Bath's just posh an borin, so no one cares about
there anyway

We spent like, six hours gettin ready round Gems
Worth it though right?!
Tunes on. Pre drinks
Stole three bottles of her mum's Echo Falls out the cupboard
Filled them back up with blackcurrant squash after, she
won't have a clue

*'Tipsy' by J-Kwon plays.*

We're in the queue, for Karma

Get ID'd on the way in, not a problem mate
Stole Dior's provisional before I came out didn't I
Dior's me sister, but we literally look nothin alike
Thank god. Different dads
Bouncers barely look at it anyway, too busy eyein up some
year 8 girls smokin at the bus stop opposite
Dior will go absolutely mental when she finds out
She's already not speakin to me since I got with her ex-
boyfriend at a house party

Not bein funny but he came on to me and they'd already
been split up for like three days

Anyway, ain't no one ruinin my vibes tonight

Tonight is my night!

So me an Gem walk in the club like we fuckin own it right

Three cider an blacks
Six sambucas later

*'Pretty Green Eyes' by Ultrabeat plays.*

TUNE!

TYRONE MILLER takes my hand! An pulls me onto the
dancefloor
Topless Tyrone, they call him, cause he's usually topless

He's like five, six years older than me, used to hang out with
my brother Daz
They were in year 11 when I was like, in year seven
Fell out big time a few years ago cause Daz slept with his
missus or somethin

Gem sees
She'll be well jealous, she's fancied him for ages
Me an Gem are bezzies, girl code an all that
But nothin's ever happened between em, so fuck it!

I stand in front of Tyrone, my booty rubbin hard into his
Well, you know
An we grind like no one's watchin
Proper sexy MTV Base kinda grindin
Not Channel U, my sister's cheap slutty mates that can't
dance are in my music video kinda grindin
No I'm talkin MTV Base slutty meets classy kinda grindin
An in that moment I feel like the most beautiful girl in . . .
Chippenham
Like this is some Save The Last Dance kinda shit

Tyrone pushes me up against the mirrors on the wall
Puts his hand up my dress. An feels right inside me
Right there on the dancefloor. Pushes himself hard inside me

Are people watchin?
Course they are.
Probably textin his girlfriend tellin her
Jealousy that's what it is
But I don't give a shit
It feels too fuckin good
In that moment I forget, everythin
I'm so happy I could scream. I could literally triple orgasm
right there on the dancefloor of Karma in front of everyone!

Gem grabs me an starts shoutin in my face, she's done so
much of her Mum's base that she's literally frothin at the
mouth, callin me a dirty slag, tellin me to get off her man

What the actual fuck?!
Seriously, she's never even said two words to the guy in
her life
I told you, it's cause she's jealous innit
Just cause I'm skinnier than her and more people fancy me
How's that my fault?

Do I listen to her?
Do I fuck?

Tyrone pulls me out the club so fast I nearly floor it right
there in front of everyone

But he catches me
Saves me
From Gem
From the shame of fallin over
From . . .
Everythin

This is the BEST night of my life
Like a really good dream, but real, like real life
We can still hear Gem shoutin after us

An we're laughin so hard
Properly creasin up
I take my shoes off
An we run

Faster
An faster
An faster

Past Charcoal Grill
Across the town bridge
Into the underground car park
The cold air hittin my skin
Tyrone Miller's hand in mine
Holdin it
Tight
My heart
Beatin
Fast
Right outta my chest
I feel

ALIVE

Like this is how life should be all the time
Not just in dreams

ALIVE
EXCITIN
SAFE

## 2 – Car Park

Tyrone clocks two boys leant against the railin's
They look familiar
I know their faces, but not their names
You never see no new faces round here

The short stocky one looks like a pitbull on steroids, not
my style
But the taller one, he's actually pretty fit
Don't get me wrong he's not Topless Tyrone Miller kinda fit
But it's good to keep your options open an all that
An it probably won't happen, but in case me an Tyrone do
ever get divorced
Then this guy might be good back up material

Tyrone pulls me towards him. An kisses me. Like proper.
Like full on tongues me for ages in front of the two boys

I hear their voices
Somethin about chlamydia
But I just ignore it
It's not true anyway
I swear down
They're just annoyed
Cause I don't fancy them

Tyrone chucks me up against the railin. Pulls up my dress.
An fucks me. Proper hard

I feel dizzy. Breathless
Like when you're really high
But not I'm gonna whitey kinda high
No, no proper dreamy kinda high

*'I Believe I Can Fly' by R. Kelly plays.*

Like . . . like . . .

'I believe I can fly' kinda high

I'M FLYIN
I'M ACTUALLY FLYIN

The boys are just stood there, watchin. Perves
'Let's have a go on your gal Tyrone'
They're comin over
The big one grabs my shoulders
'Uh don't touch what you can't afford'
He's grips me. Harder
He's actually not that fit close up
He's got a proper pissed off lookin face
Like I'm talkin Gordon Ramsay meets Ricky Hatton on
fight night
Like proper hard lookin
He's pushin his face towards mine
His lips on mine
I try an get him off me
I don't want Tyrone to think that I want him. I don't
I push him hard
Now that gets him pissed off
I can see the anger in his eyes
His muscles tensin
Clenchin
He . . .

Tyrone pulls him off me an pushes him proper hard

He stumbles backwards. Smacks into the railin's
Tyrone Miller my hero
I can't believe Tyrone Miller is stickin up for me!
This is the best night ever

The pitbull guy smacks Tyrone square in the jaw
He hits the floor
Crack
His head smashes against the concrete

The Angry Guy pulls himself from the railin's. An runs at
Tyrone
Rage
Kickin him
An kickin him
They punch

An kick
An punch
An . . .

NOOOO
STOP IT!
GET OFF HIM
PLEASEEEE
GET OFF HIM

Not my Tyrone
I scream
An scream
Pull at them
Grab at them
Scream at them

At anyone that's listenin

But no one's listenin

For once in this town, no ones listenin
The next moments flash past but sorta freeze in time
Tyrone lays there
Broken
Bloodied
Still

They turn
To me

Look
Grab
Drag

Look
Grab
Drag

Pull
Scream
Scratch

10  DESTINY

Pull
Scream
Scratch
Scratch

Black

## 3 – Hospital

*'Bound 4 da Reload' by Oxide & Neutrino plays.*

Later that night
Hospital
RUH, Bath

No A&E in Chippenham no more
Closed down
Still a maternity ward
Like, you can be born there
But if you're gonna die they ain't interested

I been checked over by the nurse
I'm sat on the ward. Waitin

Mum turns up
She's chattin away to the nurse. Whisperin
But like loud pretend whisperin
Like they do on EastEnders. So you can still hear what
they're sayin
Like prime example Stacey Slater, silly bitch, Bradley
definitely knows you're cheatin on him with his dad, Max,
cause he can hear you 'whisperin' other side of the room
about how much you were lovin his ginger pubes in your
mouth last night
You might as well just talk normal

Mum's goin on
'She brought it on herself, so don't feel sorry for her'
She comes down to my level. Right in my ear
'You stupid little cow. Look what you've done. You've really
fuckin had it this time'
Pretend whisperin again
Fake smilin at the nurse
Thinkin she can't hear her
She can
She looks away
Says nothin

Mum
Mum?
It wasn't like that
I try to explain
Tell her what happened . . .

(*Flashback.*)
Look
Grab
Drag

Look
Grab
Drag

But she's off, with the nurse
Down the corridor
Through the doors
Out the ward

Mum?
Mum!

She ignores me
Dun't look back

I look round the ward
I'm half expectin Charlie from Casualty to stroll past in his
blue uniform
He doesn't

Diamante's sat over there, my little sister
Wearin my J.Lo Sweetface velour tracksuit
My favourite fuckin tracksuit
Sly little bitch
Me an Gem nearly got nicked robbin it from House of
Frazer in Swindon

Mum's back, with the doctor now
Flirtin, touchin his arm
'I tell you Dr I've had it up to here with her. I've told her I
can't help her if she dun't help herself'

Oh here we go
Playin the innocent
Flutterin her eyelashes, as usual
I can't watch
Sit back down. Close my eyes

*Flashback – sound.*

When I wake up
Mums gone. An Diamante
Nurse says I can go home now
My injuries are all cosmetic
That's what she calls them
Cuts
Bruises
No broken bones
Minor
'You'll be alright, rest up yeah, an stay outta trouble'

Nurse says Tyrone's got a broken jaw in six places, they're keepin him in, operatin
Gotta have metal plates in his face an everythin
But she promises he'll be OK
'It could've been a lot worse, it's lucky you rang the ambulance straight away. God knows what else they'd have done if you hadn't'

(*Flashback.*)
    NOOOO
    STOP IT
    I DON'T WANT TO
    GET OFF ME
    PLEASEEEE
    GET OFF ME

I tell her I wanna see Tyrone, make sure he's OK
'It's probably best to leave it today love, he's with his family now, he don't want no other visitors'
She's right
It's probs not the best time to meet the future in laws is it?

I look a right state
I'll go home
Get cleaned up
Come back tomorrow
'The police'll sort it, don't worry. They said they'll come
round later today, take your statement'

I got no credit
So she lets me use the hospital phone
The lady at the desk looks like Mrs Blobby, spotty an creepy
as fuck

Jordan. I'll ring Jordan, his brother'll come get me
No answer
I try again, straight to answerphone
SHIT
He knows
Turned his phone off

Gem, I'll ring Gem, her stepdad'll come
Sounds like she's with someone, laughin
Hangs up
Weird, she must still be pissed off about me gettin with
Tyrone I guess

Got no money for the bus
So I walk
Over an hour to the station
Jump the train to Chippenham
Hide in the toilets the whole way

On the platform. Strangers stare
Nothin better to do, saddos
To be fair I do look a mess
Bags under me eyes
Scratches
Fat lip
Bloody knees
I'd probably stare if I didn't know me
But fine, the thing that's annoyin right is when people do it

an try an make out they ain't
Like this old biddy on the platform is proper doggin me up
Tuttin
Shakin her head
Soon as I eyeball her
She can't handle it
Looks away
If you're gonna look at me love then FUCKIN LOOK AT
ME

I walk outta the station
Down the hill
Past Karma
Dodge the red puke on the pavement
Too many cider n blacks that is, guaranteed
Past Charcoal Grill
Across the town bridge
Into the underground car park
There's two boys leanin against the wall
My stomach flips
I grab the railin's. Steady myself
Turn back. Take the long way round
Through Monkton Park
Past the brew crew
The skate park that got knocked down, cause of noise
complaints from the posh houses
Over the train bridge
An I'm on the estate
Comin up to the Spar
There's boys outside on their BMXs
What if it's . . .?
Angry guy lives . . . right there
I walk past. Fast
Head down
Don't look at them
They shout
Oi chlamydia
Chlamydia

Chlamydia
I go to run
My legs won't . . .
I walk as fast as I can
Don't look back
An I'm on the hill
Past the burnt out garages
Gem's house
With her stepdad's broken banger cars out front
The cornered off playground, that got set on fire last
summer
An I'm at my gate
Key in the door

Home
I'm home
SAFE
ALIVE

## 4 – Home

Twins are here
Fightin over my old Nokia 3310
Tryin to beat my high score on Snake 2
Good luck with that, 3515 I got, I'm the reignin
Chippenham champion, unbeaten for 9 months

There's loads of us right
Mum must've been like a bitch on heat
Popped us out one straight after the other
Don't stress yourself if you can't remember our names
They all begin with D
So if you forget, just call us D for short
That's what Mum does anyway
I swear it's so she don't have to remember who's who

She says its cause she's Diane
So she wanted the whole family to begin with D
So we'd feel like a proper tribe or somethin

I reckon really its cause she absolutely loves the D
She definitely does
We've all got different dads
Except the twins
Dunno how that would work really
Maybe if you sleep with two guys an they both cum in you at
exactly the same time

Mum says all our dad's names begin with D too
D for Dickhead
Dickhead 1, 2, 3, 4, 5
An there'll be plenty more where they came from, trust me

I switch on the TV
Straight to MTV

*MTV plays.*

Normally I'd be up there in front of the TV dancin along
I know all've the MTV Top 20 off by heart, all the moves
That's what I wanna be when I'm older, a backin dancer

For J.Lo, Ja Rule, R. Kelly
In all the music videos

Mum started pissin herself when I told her
Said I've got two left feet
But I'll show her
She's just jealous cause she never did nothin with her life

Miss Stanley, dance teacher at school, said I've got a proper raw talent
Was gonna do it for GCSE
But school dropped it
Cause only me an gay Conner Coleman chose it
Piss take really
Now I gotta do RE instead
Don't even believe in god
So what's the actual point?
That's all Mr Rideout bangs on about, god this, god that
Pure bloody bible basher he is
I actually said that to his face
Got suspended for two weeks didn't I
Definitely worth it though
Whole school heard about it
Got back to Jamal Thompson, fittest boy in the whole of 6th form
Went two's on his fag with me at lunch
An he let me suck him off behind the RE block, right next to Rideout's window
Said I'd been 'proper blessed by god with serious skills'
It was well romantic

MTV Cribs
Now that's more like it

*MTV Cribs plays.*

*Phone rings. Crazy Frog ringtone.*

SHIT SHIT SHIT
It's Jordan
He knows

I feel proper sick like
Sounds bad
But I hadn't given him a second thought last night
But now his name is flashin up on my screen
He's down Bournemouth at his dad's
But someone's fuckin told him about Tyrone, I swear

Jordan's kinda my boyfriend

Even though we've been together on an off since like year 7
an he feels more like a little brother to be honest
We ain't even had proper sex
He said he wants to wait until we're 16, so it'll be more
special
Special?! Bore off mate
Girl got needs ain't I

*Text message.*

It's Tyrone textin from hospital sayin when I speak to the
pigs don't tell them we had sex, only kissed, cause he's older
an I'm still 15 they might kick off about it. Three kisses!
I ain't stupid weren't of said nothin anyway

I stay here curled up on the sofa
Under the covers
Watchin MTV Cribs on repeat
Dreamin of LA mansions, Bentleys an walk in sneaker closets
Me an Tyrone loungin in our jacuzzi
Love n liquor

*Knock at the door.*

SHIT. SHIT

There's a key in the door
Mum?
Mum!

It's Jules
Mum's mate
Lives a few doors down.

Come to check if I'm alright
Bring me some turkey dinosaurs and potato smileys
My fave

Mum gave her a key
She's stayin at her new boyfriend's apparently
She's proper sound Jules
Like a proper Mum, nice, carin
She works down the family plannin clinic
Always gives me an Gem the strawberry flavoured johnnies
They taste so lush
Just like a strawberry Chupa Chup
I swear down
An if you're more of a strawberries an cream kinda gal
Well you know what you gotta do ladies

## 5 – Pigs

*'Routine Check' by The Mitchell Brothers plays.*

Five days later, the pigs show up, finally
By then the brusin's gone down, blood wiped away
But inside, there's this, this feelin
That won't go away
Spinnin round an round
Maybe Mum's right, for once
Brought it on myself
Shouldn't been with Tyrone cheatin on Jordan
Karma that's what it is
The club's even called Karma, for Christ's sake
That's a sign innit that bad things go down there

Mum's still away
But Jules sees the cop car pull up, comes straight round
They've come to take my statement
Say they've arrested Pitbull an Angry
But they're denyin everythin, blamin it on each other
Tyrone's pressin charges an I'm the only witness

I thought about keepin my mouth shut to the pigs
I'm not a grass or nothin, I'm not
But cause I'm the only witness, they say without my
testimony it'll be well difficult to get any kind of conviction
or justice for Tyrone
They reckon cause my injuries are only minor, it's best to
focus on the GBH conviction on Tyrone
'Unless there's anything else that happened Destiny, that
you're not telling us?'

*(Flashback.)*
   I DON'T WANT TO
   GET OFF ME
   PLEASEEEE
   GET OFF ME

'Destiny? Destiny?'

'Oi can you smell that? Smells like bacon to me
I could murder a bacon sarnie right now'
Pigs don't see the funny side. They ignore me after that

Then start goin on about my dad, sayin he's 'known to them'
Well good for you, cause I don't know him an I don't fuckin
wanna either
They flirt with Jules for a bit
One of them even puts his hand on her leg
Swear he'd finger her if I weren't there
Then they leave
I'm still pissin myself bout the bacon joke, should've seen the
copper's face
Fumin

I ring Gem to tell her, she'll appreciate my comedy genius
for sure
No answer
She best not be ignorin me still cause of the whole gettin off
with Tyrone thing
She's a proper drama queen that girl. We'll be bezzies again
next week, you watch.

# 6 – Connexions

Jules asks if I wanna go into town
Says she'll buy me a Chicko Land
'Deal.' I'm starvin.
Mum ain't been here for days, the freezer's bare I'm tellin ya
We all shared a Vienetta for breakfast, what Diamante
robbed from Spar, cause there weren't nothin else in

I munch straight through a chicken wrap, 6 chicken dippers,
8 hot wings, 2 large fries, garlic mayo an a Dr Pepper. Sorted

Jules says about goin Connexions, she's bein bangin on
about it for ages
'Now's the time love. You need to calm down a bit yeah. Stay
out of trouble. Get back into education. Get your
qualifications. Don't wanna be like me goin college in your
30s'

Connexion's is for straight up wastemen that ain't doin
nothin with their lives

Chardonnay Smith went Connexions an now she's got like
13 kids with 11 different Dad's, an one of her baby daddies
used to be her stepdad, sick innit?!

But without me really realisin what's happenin Jules links
her arm in mine, pulls me close
An before I know it, we've walked down to the town bridge
Past Shoestrings
The taxi rank
The bookies
Round the back into Connexions car park

Jules is pointin at some lame poster in the window, with
Prince's Trust on it
The boys wearin Donnay fuckin trainers! It ain't for me Jules

Next thing this guys comin through the slidin doors goin
'Hey! Can I help you?'
More like can I help you mate
He's wearin a fuckin North Face jacket

We're in Chippenham mate not the arctic circle
I put my iPod in, pretend I'm listenin to J.Lo's the remixes album
Cause I'm from Hill Rise right and J.Lo's from the Bronx which is basically same as Hill Rise just in New York, so I can proper relate to all her songs
I can hear Jules, goin on about me bein a good dancer an wantin to get on some dance course

Jules is beggin me to take my headphones out
'Just listen to what he's got to say. Hear what your options are yeah? His name's Rick, he's alright, he's here to help you'
Rick? Dick more like
I bet he's some stuck up dickhead with a degree, that buys loadsa bullshit books he never reads, to make himself look brainy. Then tries tellin me how to live my life
Fuck that!
I gotta get out of here

Dick's shovin some leaflet all up in my face
Somethin about a week long street dance course I can do in Swindon, an they'll pay my train fare. The girl on the leaflet's wearin Shox an a proper classy velour tracksuit

So I'm thinkin, alright, might not be too bad
When is it?
Next week?
Nah I'm busy then, J.Lo wants me to be the main dancer in her new vid with Ja Rule
Jules is hittin me. Tellin me to shut up
Chill out
Fuckin child abuse
Alright alright I'll do your shitty dance school if it'll shut you both up, an you give me the money for a Maccie's everyday at lunch

*'Scandalous' by Mis-Teeq plays.*

## 7 – Trial

On the train
To Swindon
Stood up
No spare seats is there
You're lucky First Great Western, that on this occasion didn't buy a ticket did I?
If I had I'd be straight up demandin a refund right now
Do I look like some mug that pays a fortune to stand up on a train?
Jog on mate

After the week long dance course. Rick got me a place on a longer one, it's every Monday night. I know all the MTV routine's now!
It's weird, but it turns out Rick's actually alright
He likes decent music. He agrees with me Dizzee is way better than Wiley
An he's got sick trainers. Air Max 90s.
He's actually not that bad lookin for an older guy
I have a session with Rick every Tuesday afternoon, check in with how it's goin
An he's helpin me with applyin for college, I'm gonna do a BTEC in Performin Arts!

I gotta miss my session this week though cause of the court case
Rick said it's best for me to focus on that

It's today
Felt like forever
Gotta go Swindon cause it's got a Crown Court
Pigs said that means it's for more serious crimes, like you see on The Bill
Stabbin's, gang rape, teacher peados, all the classics

Already got cancelled once cause some big case came in just before
This farmer guy right, near Calne got caught bummin his

pigs an chickens
Beastiality they call it, it's when humans fancy animals, it's
actually a thing that loadsa people are into
Like go down Chippenham library, they got a whole porn
section just for beastiality, trust me, they have
Look he knows, he's always down there gettin the latest
Farm Sex Porno

I jump the barriers
Walk outta the station
Through the tunnel
Into the court carpark

My mum ain't comin
Jules is though instead, she's meetin me at the court
I ain't seen my mum since she moved in with Dickhead
Dave, the new 'stepdad'
Near Newport or somethin
Said she wanted a fresh start
A fresh start in Newport?!
Please! I thought Chippenham was a shit hole, but at least
you can understand what we're sayin. I swear they don't
even speak proper English in Newport

Mum took Danny, Diamante an the twins with her
Said I'm a grown up, now that I'm 16. Old enough to look
after myself
Council put me in Avonside, temporary accommodation
down by the river
It looks like a prison. I swear. Loadsa small rooms. Bars on
the windows
Mum promised she'd come back for the trial though
Then this mornin she rings sayin somethin's come up
'You'll be fine girl. Proper tough cookie you are'
I was about to say, cookies crumble pretty easily actually, but
she'd already put the phone down

*Text message.*

It's Jordan
'You go girl! Good luck an break a leg'
Break a leg? Seriously?!
He's an idiot sometimes that boy. As if I'm about to play
Mary in the school nativity
He's stayin at his dad's for a bit down Bournemouth
His dad wouldn't let him come with me today
Says Jordan's too good for me
Whatever, I reckon really it's cause he actually fancies me
himself
He did try it on with me once, ages ago at Jord's like 13th
birthday party
Followed me into the toilet, shoved his hand down my pants,
I was in shock, didn't know what to do, so I just let him
didn't I?
Jokes! Did I fuck? I gobbed in his face, smacked him in the
balls an told him to fuck right off, or I'll tell Jord's mum

Across the car park. Gettin out of a blacked out beemer. I see
her

*'Always on Time' by Ja Rule ft. Ashanti plays.*

I knew she'd always have my back
Made a pact didn't we in year 3
BFFs. Best Friends Forever
Still wear our necklace. Never taken it off.

'Thanks for comin innit
How you been? Means a lot like you bein here
So much been goin on right. Like you know I'm livin down
Avonside now, well this proper fit guy's just moved in next
door from Bristol . . .'

She's starin straight past me
Says nothin
I get it. She wants me to say sorry first, that's what it is. She's
always been like this. Stubborn

'Babe I'm sorry. Sorry for gettin with Tyrone even though I
knew you liked him

I sent you a load of messages sayin sorry, dunno if you got
them? Who needs boys when we got each other, yeah?
I've missed you Gem
Gem?'

The driver seat door of the beemer swings open
My stomach flips
I feel sick
Dizzy

Why's Gem with . . .?

He's walkin round the car
Comin over
SHIT
I back away
He laughs. Stares right at me
The next moments flash past but sorta freeze in time

The Pitbull Guy grabs Gem
Pull her towards him. An kisses her

Gem
My best mate, since year 3
My Jenny from the block
Is here with . . . nah, it ain't right

I feel dizzy
Breathless
Like when you're really high
But not R. Kelly I believe I can fly kinda high
No, no proper I'm gonna whitey kinda high

I turn
Run out the car park
Through the tunnel
And into

It's Jules
She hugs me. Tells me how brave I am
Tells me I got this. I just gotta tell them what happened, get
those bastards sent down and then I can move on from this

whole bloody thing. Get on with my life
She says she's proud of me

Jules is right
I fuckin got this. Fuck them. Fuck Gem
I gotta do it, for Jules
An Tyrone. Can't let him down can I?
I'll get them sent down, where they fuckin belong
Then you watch Gem come crawlin back to me

I hold my head high
Me an Jules walk back through the car park, past Gem an
Pitbull
Through the slidin doors into Swindon Crown Court

An then I'm here in front of, them
Angry, Pitbull
Gem, Jules
Tyrone, he's lookin fit! Gives me the eye
Loadsa blokes in funny old fashioned wigs an like vampire
capes
Why they wearin that weird fancy dress shit?
I wanna ask, but no one seems to be laughin
Look dead serious, sorta scary actually

Jules said it would be hard, but fuck me, I feel like I'm the
criminal on the stand

The Funny Wig Guy keeps makin out I'm a liar
Sayin I had sex with Tyrone
Cause I was pissed
Nah, I never
Sayin I'm protectin him
Sayin Pitbull an Angry were protectin me
That Tyrone was takin advantage of me
Nah, I like Tyrone I swear
They're twistin my words
Talkin about Tyrone bein older
I wanted to
Wanted to what Destiny?

Tyrone's starin at me
Pitbull. Angry. Smilin
Nah. Nah. I WANTED TO HAVE SEX WITH TYRONE

Tyrone looks pissed
Shakin his head
Everyone's starin at me
Callin me a liar
Sayin I'm an unreliable witness
Cause I lied in my statement about not havin sex with
Tyrone
Sayin I brought all this on myself
Cause of what I was wearin
Cause I'd had three cider an blacks
Cause I was walkin home with a boy, an older boy
Cause of who my dad is
Cause of where I live
Cause my brothers are trouble
Oh yeah, they've heard about me
Basically it must've been my fault cause I'm me, Destiny

The wig guys sayin it was rape. If I'm tellin the truth. Tyrone
was rapin me, cause I was underage
Tyrone stands up
Goes to leave
Pitbull's laughin
Gem's smilin at him
Tyrone's walkin out

Then I say it
I just say it
What happened
Everythin

I tell them what they did to me. What Pitbull an Angry did

Look
Grab
Drag

Look
Grab
Drag

GET OFF ME
PLEASEEE
GET OFF ME

NO
STOP IT
I DON'T WANT TO

Pull
Scream
Scratch
Scratch

Black


They say I'm lyin again
They say no further questions

## 8 – Avonside

Couple of days later this social worker turns up Avonside
There's this posh lady behind her wearin a suit!
She looks well serious
I'm thinkin who the fuck's she an what's she doin round
here lookin like that?
Says she wants a chat with me downstairs in the meetin room
Reckons she's a pig, but she ain't got no uniform on

Pig lady's goin on about what happened at the trial
I don't wanna fuckin talk about it if I'm honest
I'm done with it. Everyone's been chattin shit about me
since, it's gone round the whole of this place already
The skanks downstairs locked me in the shower block last
night, wouldn't let me out till I said I made it all up

Pig lady says Angry an Pitbull have been acquitted
Been what?
That the case against them has been chucked out of court,
cause of me an Tyrone lyin in our statements, an Tyrone's
decided to drop the charges

She's goin on about the seriousness of the allegations I made
against Angry an Pitbull, what I said they did to me
How she needs to follow it up
An do I wanna talk to her about it?
Tell her what really happened?

Nah. Do I fuck? I made it all up anyway
She's askin me if that's definitely the case. Did it happen or
not Destiny? Tell me the truth.
I just told you I made it up. It never fuckin happened
She's starin at me. Suspicious like

Hands me some business card, DCI Holmes from Wiltshire
Police
Shut the front door! As in Detective Holmes? Where's
Watson to?
I can see her smirkin. She's tryin not to laugh. Says to give
her a call if I wanna talk. Yeah whatever

I run upstairs, grab a bottle of vodka from my room
An I down the fucker in one
Tastes like shit
But good shit
Yeahhh. Good shit

*She downs a bottle of vodka.*

**9 – Aftermath**

*Phone rings.*

I wake up

It's Jules. Fifteen missed calls! I ain't spoke to her since the trial. Since I fucked it all up. Let everyone down, her, Tyrone, Mum . . .

*Knock on the door.*

'Destiny. Come on love, I know you're in there'

I get up, slowly
So I don't puke
Open the door

It's Rick!
He looks, nice
He's askin if I'm alright?
Says he wanted to see how I'm doin
Cause I missed my session this week
He's askin me how the trial went?

'Amazin yeah. Just glad it's over innit. Don't think about it no more or nothin. I feel fuckin good. Never better really'

Shiiit
I puke all over his new Shell Toes
He'll be fumin
'They're only shoes sweetheart an it'll come off'

'Come an see me tomorrow yeah. We gotta get all your forms filled out for college in time. You don't wanna lose your place now do you?'

## 10 – Rick

I see Rick twice a week now
On Tuesdays an Thursdays

An we sorta get on
He's actually pretty sound to be fair
I tell him things. Stuff I never even told Gem or Jules. An he
propcr listens. Dun't judge, just listens

As the weeks go on I start thinkin, I can change things.
Rick says he's here for me, to help get my life on track
He says they've stopped doin the Performin Arts course at
Chippenham college, but I can go Trowbridge college instead
He sorts me out a free bus pass cause he knows someone
what works for the council
Says after college I can go to a proper dance school in
London, he'll help me with the application
Rick says I'm a really talented dancer, that he knows I'm
gonna make it as a professional
He gets me to show him all my new routines, says he loves
watchin me dance
That my rhythm an natural talent is proper inspirin
He says I've taught him things he didn't even know
Rick says I can make my own destiny, that I'm a good person
an I deserve to be happy

He helps me get a part time job at Maccies, takin the orders
on the drive thru, he helped me with the application an we
did loadsa roleplays before my interview
It's not the LA dream, but I get free Big Macs an it means I
can save money an buy all the proper dance stuff I need for
the course, gotta get leotards, ballet, tap shoes, all that shit
Obviously I don't wanna be a ballet dancer or nothin, but
ballet's actually the basis of all dance styles, even like the
dutty wine

September comes round well quick, an I start college an the
course is actually pretty sick
The bus journey's a proper mission, but it'll be worth it

though right
Jessica Alba will be callin me any day now, askin me to be in
Honey 2

Rick's right ya know, things are lookin up!

Me an Rick. We start fallin for each other. Like properly,
fallin for each other
I've literally never felt this way about anyone before
Now I know what true love feels like

All those wasters before
That was definitely not love

Rick though. Big difference
He knows, about love, life. Everythin
He feels the same. He holds me. Looks right in my eyes
Says 'I've been waitin my whole life to meet you. Nothin has
ever felt so right'

Rick says it's more special if we keep it just between us
Like a secret, like somethin sacred we have what no one else
knows about
He says that makes it more excitin too. Like a game that only
we can play
That only we know the rules too

I ain't told Jules yet
Cause he's a bit older than me
An some people might say it's wrong cause I'm only sixteen
But in the words of Aaliyah 'Age ain't nothing but a number'
right?
An Aaliyah knows cause her an R. Kelly were in love. An
people said he was a paedo
Cause she was only, 15 when they got married an he was
like, nearly 30
But those people were just jealous an had obviously never
been in love before
Not true love like ours. Like R. Kelly an Aaliyah kinda love

We have the best sex
I used to think you couldn't even have sex once you're over
30
Gem used to say it was illegal. Cause you're too wrinkly.
You're bits stop workin
But Rick is really good
Like not just goin through the motions
Thinkin about what you're gonna have for dinner. Or
fantasizin about Lizo from Newsround goin down on you

Na with Rick its like properly makin love
You don't need to be thinkin about Lizo or no one else
It's, romantic. Like, you see in the films
We do it at Avonside always. I have to sneak him in through
the back fire exit. He says 'At Connexions we gotta act like
normal. Like nothin's goin on between us'
But sometimes he touches my leg under the table or brushes
past me way too close. An it's like, lightnin, like there's
electricity between us about to explode or somethin
He says 'We gotta be careful, we need to play it safe. We can't
be seen out an about together, not yet'
Soon though, we're gonna tell everyone about us
Then we'll be together all the time
Just me an Rick
I get proper butterflies thinkin about our life together
I feel, excited
Alive
Safe

Rick makes me feel safe

## 11 – Final Session

Todays my final session at Connexions
Rick said somethin about fundin cuts an now I'm 16, started
college, got a job an that. I can't really get help no more
So I dress up all nice. Make a proper effort for Rick. Get to
Connexions
When I go in Rick's bein, distant. He won't even look at me.
I get it. He's nervous cause we agreed we're gonna tell
everyone about us soon. He's worried he'll lose his job, that
people will be weird about it

So I don't get upset, or try it on with him
I act like a proper big woman
I just walk out. Give him some space

I gotta plan see

But I gotta act fast
I peg it up the hill to the station. Jump the train to Swindon
I know where I'm headin
Straight there. The place that keeps relationships alive

Ann Summers, Swindon High Street
She should be knighted really by the Queen. Amount of
relationships she must've saved

Me, Rick an Ann Summers. Like some beautiful romantic
threesome
I've always wanted a proper threesome
Me an Gem did try it once in year 5 with her older brother,
Bradley, in the Brewers Fayre Ball Pool Pit, it was proper
weird
Bradley got a bit over excited to say the least
Puttin his hands here there an everywhere
There was balls flyin all over the shop, not his, no like the
plastic ones

Straight to the fancy dress section
One slutty nurse's outfit please Ann

Tonight I'm gonna look after my man. Take real good care
of him

Open my bag
Slutty nurse outfit. Bag
Rampant Rabbit. Bag
Toffee sauce. Bag
Crotchless lace knickers. Bag
Sorted

I make a dash for it
Out the door
Alarm goes off
Don't look back
I run. Faster an faster
This is gonna be the best night ever

Back in Chippenham
I wait for Rick outside Connexions
There he is
I duck behind a car
Don't want him to see me
Want it to be a proper surprise
Worked it all out like
He'll get in his car
I'll jump in a taxi on the rank, get the driver to follow him
I dunno what car he's got. Bet it's a Benz, or a Bentley
It's weird we're in love, an I don't even know what car he
drives or where he lives
Will tonight though
I'll probably move into his place soon
Me an Rick
Loadsa babies
A proper family. Like a real one

Wait! He's crossin the road, to the bus stop?
The X31 pulls up
He goes up to the top deck
I jump on. Sit at the back downstairs

I'm buzzin. You wait till he sees my outfit, he won't be able to keep his hands off me

We're on the bus for ages!
Past Sainsbury's
Cepan Park, the posh new estate
Out of Chippenham
He must live in Bath
Bet he's proper minted!
Everyone in Bath's a millionaire, smallest house you can get, 26 bedrooms

Into Corsham
Past Co-op
The Texaco garage
Through Potley estate
Which is basically Hill Rise, but in Corsham
Into Box

Shit. He's comin downstairs
I jump off

Past the village hall. The church
He opens the gate, to a cottage, pretty like you get on Heartbeat
Key in the door, he's goin inside
It's not quite a Bath mansion, but still it looks nice for an old place

Outside his door
My heart beatin. . .

Final spray of Impulse Tease
Slutty nurse's outfit
Crotchless knickers
Rampant rabbit
Not sure where to hold it
The mouth
Not in the mouth
Touchin the lips
Sexy like

Hair
Lip gloss
Doorbell
The door opens

A woman answers
Holdin a baby. There's a toddler grabbin at her feet
'Hello, can I help you?'
I stare at her
Speechless

*Breakdown movement sequence.*

*She loses her shit.*

## 12 – Hope

It's been a couple of months since what happened, with
Rick, at his house
I proper lost it apparently, flipped out
Last thing I remember is lobbin the rampant rabbit through
Rick's kitchen window, nearly knocked his wife out

Pigs picked me up on the bypass near Bath
Half naked, shoutin at the traffic

Jules says I shouldn't beat myself up about it
She says it's not surprisin I freaked out after everythin what
happened with, Angry, Pitbull an then. . .

Rick denied everythin
Our whole relationship
Said that I made it all up
That it was some fantasy in my head
Which ain't true
It did happen. I swear

There's some investigation happenin or somethin by the
pigs, I think.
That's what Mel said. Mel's my social worker. I got like my
own one now
She's actually pretty nice. She's not like one of them weird
kiddie snatcher ones
She says I gotta stay away from Rick. I ain't allowed to see or
contact him

Had to have all these chats after with all these different
grown ups about what happened They was all well serious
One of them was that Sherlock Holmes lady that came down
Avonside
Mel was always there with me though, so it weren't that bad
She'd bring me Dr Pepper, Pom-Bears, Wham Bars, all my
favorite snacks

Moved into a new place now ain't I?
It's in Trowbridge. Right near the college

It's like a house for teenagers, there's an adult what works
there, that checks what we're doin now an then, but we can
do what the fuck we want most of the time
It's actually a proper nice yard
Well for Trowbridge anyway
I got an ensuite with my own toilet an a shower, I know
right, ballin
I'll be on MTV Cribs next week, you watch

Jules comes to see me most Saturdays
Takes me down the Shires for a Boswells or Shakeaway
She says she's proper proud of me. How well I'm doin
She brought me a fridge magnet the other day, for my fridge
It say's 'We're all in the gutter but some of us are looking at
the stars'
Deep innit
Think like 2Pac wrote it or somethin

A couple of weeks after I moved to Trowbridge, this new girl
moved into the house from Melksham
Faith she's called
Now I don't usually like Melksham girls to be honest, they're
proper chavvy
But Faith she ain't like that, she's proper classy, from Bower
Hill, the new estate, it's like Beverley Hills but in Melksham
She grew up in foster care or somethin. But then her foster
mum got a new boyfriend an he started sayin weird flirty
stuff to Faith, she told her foster mum an she didn't believe
her, so she had to move out

It sounds a bit lame but we actually bonded over Teenage
Mutant Ninja Turtles
She's like proper obsessed with them, but in a cool way. Like
she just likes what she likes
Don't give a shit about what people think of her, that's what I
like about her I guess

First day she moved in right, she stormed over, proper
bolshy, like she might twat me one, grabbed my arm an
pulled me into her room

I was about to fuckin nut her one
Then I looked round, saw them all lined up, turtle figures
everywhere, hundreds of them, like proper rare ones, some
still in the box, never been opened
I couldn't speak. I was kinda like starstruck. I literally loved
the turtles as a kid!

Turns out Faith's well good at singin an rappin
So we've started a girl group called, Teenage Ninja Girls or
TNG
In honour of the turtles an TLC
Faith knows some big record producer in Swindon that used
to be Biggie's manager before he got shot an he's gonna help
us get a deal

We're auditionin this new girl later for Teenage Ninja Girls.
She moved in yesterday
She is from Potley in Corsham!
But we'll give her a chance I guess
She better not turn up in Donnay fuckin trainers though I'm
tellin ya
She's called Hope, which is a bit lame, but I guess it could
work . . .

Destiny. Faith. Hope.


*The End.*


*'Waterfalls' by TLC plays.*